FINDING
PEACE IN THE
STORM

A 30 DAY DEVOTIONAL TO ENCOURAGE WOMEN WHO ARE EXPERIENCING SEPARATION AND/OR DIVORCE

KENDRA S. GRISSOM

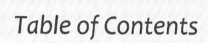

Table of Contents

INTRODUCTION

Following the Will of God During Marriage Separation

Can you think of a time in your life when everything seemed to be going well but in an instant everything changed? It has been said that the only constant in life is change and by extension, uncertainty. We create patterns and habits that we want to define in our lives but then out of nowhere life throws us a curveball. For many unfortunate marriages that curveball begins with separation and sometimes ends in divorce. If this is or was your experience, I can assure you; you are not alone. Every situation that we encounter is for a reason and all things work together for good (Romans 8:28). This devotional is for those who want to walk through divorce feeling empowered and loved. Upon completing this devotional you will come out on the other end with a clear mind and a guilt-free heart. *How do I know? This devotional was birthed while separated which led to a divorce. Unaware of what the outcome would be I depended on the Holy Spirit to help me daily.*

Each day will begin with scripture so you can fight against the enemy that comes to steal your joy. Remember that God can turn your situation around and place you on top by His grace. We must go directly to Him with our troubles and allow Him to heal our brokenness. I encourage you to document how you feel each day. Pay close attention to each feeling that you encounter throughout the day and keep a journal to track your progress. Write down revelations you receive as well as the things you are thankful for. Don't leave out your thoughts and feelings that stood out to you also. At the end of your 30 days, reflect on how you were when you first began. Then recognize the growth you have achieved. I pray that this devotion will give you the push that you need to allow our Father God to restore your life greater than it has ever been.

Before moving into the devotional I would like to give you the opportunity to accept Jesus as your Savior. If your answer is **YES** you can express your belief and trust in Jesus through this simple prayer.

Father God, I know that my sins separated me from you. Thank you for sending Jesus Christ to die on the cross for my sins so that I can have eternal life. Jesus forgive me for my sins and come into my heart. Lord, I ask that you direct my path forevermore in Jesus name, Amen.

I would like to welcome you into God's family, sister. I pray that the Holy Spirit works inside of you as He has worked inside of me! Amen!

Day 1

The Problem

Psalms 81:6 "Now I will take the load from your shoulders; I will free your hands from their heavy tasks."

The sad truth is more Christians today are experiencing separation and divorce. See, the unfortunate reality of life is that it presents us with a set of challenges. Sometimes, we wish there was a button we could press to make it all disappear. However, life is not that easy. It seems as if we manage to solve one problem and then another one is almost always right around the corner.

Scripture reminds us that there is no problem that God cannot handle. However, when we are faced with adversity God sometimes becomes our last resort. Perhaps you do not have a job, money is low, and you are now on your own again after years of being married. Perhaps you have all the finances in the world but your heart is too full and your burdens are too heavy for you to properly enjoy it. Wherever you fall it is up to you to decide that you will not let this yoke around your neck paralyze you. Take your problems to the Lord and lay them at his feet.

The Bible says in James 1:2-4, "Consider it pure joy, my brothers and sisters, whenever you face trials of many kinds, because you know that the testing of your faith produces perseverance. Let perseverance finish its work so that you may be mature and complete, not lacking anything." The path to joy will have many obstacles, problems are promised, but so is God's grace. The first step is acknowledging that the situation exists, laying it at the feet of Jesus, and trusting that He will do the rest.

Additional reading: (James 1:2-4; Psalms 55:22; Matthew 11:28)

1. What are a few things that have been troubling your mind lately?

2. Name a few things that can be seen as positive in this situation.

3. Write out a detailed plan to help you rid yourself of each of the things that trouble you.

Day 2

Taming The Anger

"Proverbs 14:29 People with understanding control their anger; a hot temper shows great foolishness."

God knows that separation comes with a lengthy list of emotions. Anger, hurt, pain, regret, and so many feelings that can sometimes turn into weapons. Anger is a natural emotion. The problem lies in dwelling on it and not managing it effectively. God knows that when we operate in the flesh we can allow anger to control our actions however he warns us Ephesians 4:2 that even in anger we should "sin not."

Anger damages earthly relationships as well as threatens our relationship with God. If you allow this unhealthy form of anger, that is controlled by satan, to control you then that anger will leak over into your relationship with God. You will then find yourself blaming God for your separation or divorce, however, the emotional scars of divorce can only be healed by God. Anger will allow you to feel entitled to vengeance and/or retribution but God's love will allow us to feel entitled to passing grace. Grace is what God gives us although we don't deserve it.

While separated, I had episodes of anger, bitterness, and resentment towards my spouse. At times, my anger would allow me to curse him but yet I yearned for peace. I made the decision not to allow bitterness to control my day to day thoughts and actions any longer. I began praying for peace over my life and my situation. I asked God to remove any bitterness and resentment from my heart so I could fully focus my time on Jesus.

When going through difficult times anger can be an overpowering feeling however God's love is even more powerful. Begin petitioning God for a heart of forgiveness and allow it to flow freely. As you allow God to overflow your heart with love allow yourself to forgive you as well as others.

Additional reading: (Psalms 37:8; Proverbs 29:22; Ecclesiastes 7:9)

1. What are the thoughts that you feel when the spirit of anger comes upon you?

2. Write those thoughts down, pray against them, and leave them at Jesus feet. Do this daily if needed!

Day 3

Forgiveness

Ephesians 4:32 "Be kind and compassionate to one another, forgiving each other, just as in Christ forgave you."

Blaming your spouse is easy to do when separated or going though a divorce but the hardest thing to do is pass forgiveness. Sometimes people emotionally and/or physically cut us so deep that we'll rather cut them back instead of forgiving. Harboring resentment only affects you while the other person has moved on with their life. As Christ followers, we are called to forgive others without buts. God commanded us to forgive and furthermore, he didn't create an exclusion clause for spouses or former spouses. His instructions are the same to us as they are for everyone else. If we rely on our own strength and our fleshly desires, this can become problematic. Unforgiveness leads to hatred and hatred keeps us isolated from God.

There are a few things to remember about forgiveness:

1. Forgiveness is not a vanishing potion. Forgetting is physically and humanly impossible. However, we can

choose to release the bitterness associated with the memories.

2. The process of forgiving begins when you decide to forgive. This step isn't easy however pray and ask God to help you forgive. When we are betrayed trust is broken, feelings are hurt, insecurities are paraded, and everything feels like a mess. Life seems to be in shambles and the pain just won't go away. This is why it's important to allow the Holy Spirit to mend your brokenness and to teach you how to forgive. We must work toward forgiveness every single day.

3. Forgiveness is a gift to you first before it is a gift to anyone else. When we hoard bitterness and unforgiveness in our hearts, we make ourselves physically and spiritually sick. When it begins to fester, we start to experience aches and pains all over our body and we lose the authentic connection to heaven. If we recall the Lord's prayer, we will realize that unforgiveness prevents us from receiving forgiveness. How much are we in need of our Savior's grace daily? How often do we sin? If we choose not to forgive, we pile our transgressions at the doorway of our heart, refusing to grant God entry.

4. There is no one on earth worth your salvation. God is an understanding and forgiving God. He wants us to be sincere with Him as He already knows our hearts. As we are walking through dark times he desires to guide us through. Today, make the decision to forgive and allow God to do the rest.

Additional reading: (Matthew 6:14; Mark 11:25; Luke 17:3)

1. Make a list of the situations or people that seem too hard to forgive.

2. Pray specifically for God to help you to make peace with those situations and people.

3. Reflect on ways that you have been unkind to yourself and then forgive yourself.

Day 4

Let Go And Let God

Exodus 14: 14 "The Lord will fight for you; you need only to be still."

I was going through a very rough time and I found it difficult to sit back and just let God fight for me. It seemed that everything around me was crumbling right before my eyes. I started thinking about my children, and how the separation was affecting them. "I have not worked in 10 years, so where do I go from here?" "Who wants to marry a woman with four kids?" "Who wants to marry a woman that has been married twice already?" "Would I even want to marry me?" So many thoughts crowded my mind, I could hardly function properly. Then God told me to call my sister in Christ. While speaking to her, she said, "The Lord will fight for you, just stay calm." I knew right away, God was speaking directly to me. As I sat and contemplated, I realized that God was telling me to SHUT MY MOUTH AND ALLOW HIM TO WORK. The exact same thing that God had been telling me weeks leading up to the separation. Shutting up was difficult however I decided to submit myself to God's will.

15

We, as women, tend to feel as though we can fix everything on our own. Then, difficult situations like separation slaps us in the face and we learn the hard truth. We are not GOD. The Bible says we should not lean on our own understanding but turn every aspect of our lives over to God. Let your test become your testimony. This battle that you're fighting wasn't yours to begin with. It belonged to the Lord so take your gloves off and allow him to lead you into your destiny.

Additional reading: (Psalm 34:17; James 4:7; Proverbs 3: 5-6)

1. What are a few things that you can be more patient concerning right now?

2. What are some things that you can do to stay calm when you begin feeling overwhelmed? Create a plan to implement those things into your life. Remember them when you feel low.

Day 5

Finding Faith In Your Chaos

Proverbs 3:5 "Trust in the Lord with all your heart; do not depend on your own understanding."

It is not uncommon to feel alone and scared of what might happen at the next phase of your life. When everything feels chaotic and out of control, there is only one firm foundation on which we can stand. That foundation is Jesus Christ.

Do you remember the story of Jesus and his disciples in the middle of a raging sea? The disciples looked at the waves, became terrified, and then ran to Jesus. Seeing the disciples fear of what was happening, Jesus calmed the sea. He then asked them the same question that has been asked to many believers over the years, "Where is your faith?"

Faith helps us to look at the darkness engulfing the tunnel and see the light beckoning to us at the end. The light is Jesus Christ and he invites us to keep the faith. Jesus encourages us that our faith should lie only in

Him. In this hour, divorce may be the darkness threatening to consume you. However, with God's mercy, love, kindness, steadfastness, grace, and faithfulness shines brighter at the end of the tunnel. God continues to encourage us to keep pressing towards the light of His promises. He is faithful and He's an unchanging God. It's important to keep your eyes planted on God and not allow the enemy to snatch your faith away while you're going through hard times.

Additional reading: (Psalms 46:10; Hebrew 11:1; 1 Corinthians 16: 13)

1. How do you struggle in having faith during times when everything seems hopeless?

2. Name some faith builders in your life.

3. Focus on believing in God for your future and your present situations every single day.

Day 6

Healing

Psalm 34:18 "The Lord is close to the brokenhearted; he rescues those whose spirits are crushed."

When marriages fail, we tend to cling to the idea that we will never get over what happened. We sometimes question our value. While you may feel unworthy divorce is not a death sentence. If anything, it is an opportunity to be reborn and remodeled into a new creature in Christ. It is a wound that can and will be healed.

How do you begin? Everyone's story is different, but while I was separated, I decided to allow God's will to be done. If God seen fit for my marriage to end I accepted the process. I allowed God to work in me while I grieved emotionally not knowing what would be the outcome. The ending of a marriage can be akin to death (and in some cases worse than physical death). When we go through a divorce, we lose a part of ourselves. We lose the years spent in our marriage and the future we envisioned. These are all things that I began to mourn. The Bible says, "In my distress,

I called upon the Lord and cried to my God, and he did hear my cry" (Psalm 18:6). While you grieve the loss you should not live in the loss. We must muster up the strength and courage to move forward into our new beginning. Invite God into your heart to turn your despair and disappointments into building a new you. It will not happen overnight so you may find yourself seeking God like never before. It may take more praying and fasting but you'll receive the promise of healing.

Remember that God loves you and that He is willing and able to heal you. He can guide you through the healing process if you let Him. You'll be glad you did.

Additional reading: (Psalms 6:2; Psalms 30:2; Philippians 4:13)

1. What are some of your favorite self-care practices? Think of a few to do a few times a week and watch how you begin to feel better on a consistent basis.

2. What does healing look like for you?

3. What are your goals for the next year?

Day 7

Managing The Loneliness

John 14:16 "And I will pray to the father, and he shall give you another comforter that he may abide with you forever."

Today happens to be going well but suddenly it hits you, I'm single... again. Then the spirit of loneliness begins to set in. You may revisit overly familiar feelings of doubt, insecurity, and jealousy. Especially when you're watching movies or see other couples out in public. You may ask yourself, "Will I be alone forever?" Then, you begin to panic and build your dating profile on ImSingleAgain.com

Honey, STOP! Do not start looking for another man. Place your focus on your Father God so that He can teach you how to love yourself first. Allow God to fill your void of loneliness so you won't fall into the traps of sexual sin. Friends will tell you, "Girl, in order for you to get over him you need to get under another one." Well, I tell you to find new friends that's going to encourage you to depend on God. Take this time out for self love and implement examples listed to ease your loneliness:

21

- put your phone down and take time to listen to God's voice
- take yourself out to eat
- take a relaxing bubble bath
- join a bible study group
- get involved in church functions
- drive and take short vacations to new places
- take on a new hobby
- spontaneously do things that you've always wanted to do and so much more! The Bible says that, "the Lord will go before you, he will go with you, and he will not forsake you, so there is no need to be dismayed." (Deuteronomy 31:8) Through his Holy Spirit within, He promises to be your present help in times of need.

If you are now in the season of loneliness trust that God is with you. Everyone feels lonely at times especially after any number of years of marriage. That is okay. What you should not do is isolate yourself from others. Spend more time with your friends and family but most importantly, spend a lot more time building your relationship with God.

Additional reading: (Matthew 18:20; Isaiah 41:10; Isaiah 43:1-2)

1. Name a few things that you have always wanted to do but lacked drive or opportunity?

2. *Make a list of places that you would like to travel to and make a plan to visit one soon.*

Day 8

Relationship With God

1 Peter 5:6 *"Humble yourself, therefore under the mighty hand of God, that he may exalt you in due time."*

Have you ever felt like no matter how hard you tried and no matter what you did nothing seemed to be enough?

It's because you're depending on yourself instead of depending on God. How is your relationship with God? Do you commune with him daily? Do you divulge in His word and seek His presence during your time of trouble? Building a relationship with God requires submitting to his commands and allowing Him to be enough for you. When you decide to draw near to God then he'll draw near to you.

If you do not have a relationship with God, just know this about Him: His door is always open and your divorce does not make you any less loved by Him. He loves you with an everlasting love and not the tainted love that man gives. I'm talking about His sacrificial love he gave by choosing to die on the cross for you! Your divorce may cause you to question whether you are worthy of or capable of love but I assure you that the answer to both is yes. An effective way to start or rebuild your relationship is by reading God's word, fasting, and having daily devotion with him. Set a specific time to meet with Him and find peace in His presence.

Additional reading: (1 Peter 5:6-7; Psalms 34:17-19; Matthew 11:28)

1. Write out a plan on how you will spend time in God's presence. Ex: Wake up at 5am, pray, worship, and read the chapter of the day. Be more detailed with your plan. Also I encourage you to begin your journey with Romans 1.

Day 9

Managing The Pain

Psalms 147:3 "He heals the brokenhearted and binds up their wounds."

The ending of a relationship is one of those painful situations that more of us are facing today. Most of us are not equipped to handle this kind of emotional scarring. How do we manage the pain that comes with it? How can we alleviate the pressure building up inside us?

1. Accept the loss. Whether you initiated the divorce or received the devastating news you will have to accept the loss. After making an effort to reconcile your marriage, if the outcome is still divorce, then acceptance is key to moving on.

2. Talk to someone. Not just anyone but a Jesus follower. This person will always lead you back to the word of God. We are encouraged to fellowship with each other not just on a weekly basis but to bear each other's burdens. This implies a relationship built on trust amongst the body of Christ. Prayerfully ask the Lord to lead you to a confidant and prayer partner.

27

3. Do not rush the healing process. Give yourself time to heal.

4. Place your faith in God. In the midst of your pain put your trust in God and allow Him to heal your broken heart. Pain is inevitable and while we cannot escape it God teaches us how to release it to Him.

Additional readings: (Psalms 34:18; Jeremiah 17:14; Romans 8:18)

1. List things that you can do to make yourself feel good this week. Try to do at least one!

2. What are a few things that you like to do? Do more of that regularly.

Day 10

Do You Feel Ashamed?

Psalms 25:20 "O keep me and deliver me; let me not be ashamed; for I put my trust in thee."

Have you ever felt lost, confused, and unsure of who you really are? Shame whispers in your ears and tells you that nothing will come from your life. Then, you start to hide in your own little hole of shame.

If there was abuse of any kind in your marriage you may feel stifled by a mask of shame. Isolation seems like the best solution and you may also try to keep yourself hidden from the world. If this is you, I understand. Abuse is a torture device from the devil. It erodes our will and tears away at our confidence. It strips us of strength and destroys our trust. When you feel this way, you have to first confess your true feelings to the only One that we know we can trust— God. We take our tattered pieces to him in trembling hands and ask Him to put us back together again. There is no shame at the foot of the cross. Just exposed sinners in need of their Savior. We have to release shame as well as pride in order for us to fully receive the light of God's healing and restorative touch in our lives.

There is no shame among sinners as we have all sinned and fallen short of God's glory. He loves us all the same and sees us as lost sheep that are worth saving. You are worth saving! You are branded by God and sealed for His purpose and THAT is nothing to be ashamed of. Walk uprightly in your parentage while boldly declaring that you are and will forever be His.

Additional reading: (Ezra 9:6; Psalms 31: 1; Proverbs 11:2)

1. What situations have happened in your life that brought you shame? Go back to those situations and pray for your deliverance from our Father God in Jesus' name.

2. Declare this affirmation daily: My pain does not bring me shame. I am fearfully and wonderfully crafted by God.

Day 11:

Do You Feel Like A Failure?

Psalms 73:26 "My health may fail, and my spirit may grow weak, but God remains the strength of my heart; he is mine forever."

Never speak failure over your life because of a failed situation. Everything happens for a reason but that doesn't give cause to beat yourself up. When choosing to focus on the things that you cannot change it opens the door to becoming a victim of depression and anxiety. Fixating on your mistakes leaves you stuck in your past but choosing forgiveness allows you to focus on your present. You have to depend on the Holy spirit to help you move past your situation.

Divorce isn't always easy, however, in some cases it could be what was needed. I'm not an advocate for divorce however there are times marriages end because we chose our husband and not the husband God chose for us. So we end up in marriages that we want God to mend that he never placed together in the beginning. This may not be you but when we're not walking with

31

God we tend to make flesh moves, that in the end, make us feel like failures.

Remember, you are not a failure. Your circumstances doesn't define who you are but who you are is defined in Jesus Christ.

Additional reading: (Romans 5:3-5; John 14:1-31; Joshua 1:9)

1. Write a love letter to yourself. What do you say about yourself? How do you feel?

2. Choose an organization to volunteer with before the year is out. You may find that giving to others will give to you in an intrinsic way.

Day 12

Seek A Community

Romans 12:5 "So we being many are one body in Christ and every member one of another."

According to research, in this day and age, many Christian marriages are ending in divorce. It is an issue that is spread throughout the world, and you are definitely not alone. Going through a divorce can be really frustrating and sometimes it can be really hard to find a support system. However, you will see that there are support groups and people who are willing to give a nonjudgmental ear. As you begin to seek support you will find that there are other women going through similar situations as yours. So, you're not alone.

I can't say this enough, when seeking guidance it's important to lean on someone that's grounded in the word of God. Whether it be a local pastor or a christian counselor, they need to be able to help strengthen your faith in Jesus Christ. If you're finding it difficult to receive community help try attending a different church. Begin praying and asking God for guidance. The body of Christ is a community where you can find the fellowship and support that you need.

Do not try to handle your issues alone. Allow God to lead you to a group or person that best fits your needs.

Additional readings: (James 5:16; Matthew 18:20; 1 Peter 4:8-11)

1. Name a person that you can lean on to help combat your loneliness. Pray for God to provide them with the provision and strength to help lead you through.

2. What are a few things that you can do to comfort yourself through your lonely times?

Day 13

Talk About It

1 Peter 5:17 "Cast all your anxiety on him because he cares for you."

We can agree that in the time we live in today, many of us are afraid to talk about what happens inside of our marriages. Sometimes it is because we are too afraid or ashamed to hear what others might say. We become so trapped by silence and moving on seems like even more of an impossibility.

I can recall being afraid to communicate the things going on inside of my marriage. The enemy was keeping me trapped in silence because I was afraid of being called a failure. So I dealt with the infidelity, the pornography, blatant disrespect, severe mental and emotional abuse. Suffering in silence led to me responding with violence which lead to shame. This crippled me to remain silent knowing no one would believe that I was retaliating from being abused. Eventually I began contemplating suicide and this is when I sought out christian counseling.

Speaking about problems to the right person will not only help you but it might help someone else who is also suffering. The christian counselor taught me the word of God which lead to me obtaining salvation. If this is you, seek help! Don't allow the enemy to keep you trapped in silence another day.

Your testimony can be someone else's window to help them speak up as well.

Additional reading: (Romans 12:4-5; Matthew 7:7; Exodus 18:14-15)

1. When you begin to feel alone, who do you reach out to?

2. Make a list of confidants that you can call on to comfort you during your depressed times.

Day 14

Forget The Past

Isaiah 43:18 "Remember ye, not the former things, neither consider the things of old."

Forget the past! What do you mean forget the past? How can I forget about what they did? How can I forget the pain that they put me through? How do I move on from this?

Forgetting the past is a simple concept that is made to be complex. In this case it means to stop reliving, revisiting, and ruminating on the past. When emotions are raw and memories flood our mind, it is difficult to tune them out. Everyday, prayerfully ask the Lord to take control of your emotional responses to these painful memories. Ask Him for patience to push past the pain to see the promises that awaits you on the other side of healing.

I had been laboring under the weight of my separation. Until one day, I realized that I was allowing it to hinder me from moving into what God had for me. Allow Your Father to heal your deep woven wounds so that you can look past what caused it. Once you do that, you will open a window for God to do something new in your life.

Additional readings: (Philippians 3:13; 2 Corinthians 5:17; 2 Corinthians 5:17)

1. What prevents you from walking in forgiveness and erasing the past?

2. Task yourself to pray for forgiveness and the healing of your heart daily.

Day 15

Do Not Give Up

2 Chronicles 15:7 "Be ye strong therefore, and let not your hands be weak; for your work shall be rewarded."

One of the easiest things to do when facing difficulties is giving up and throwing in the towel. Sometimes life is like a boxing match and you are constantly getting punched and knocked down while trying to find the strength to get back up. Going through marriage difficulties can sometimes feel just like that. It can feel as if you're constantly losing a pointless battle that can be resolved but seems as though it will never be resolved.

One of my favorite Bible stories is about Job. Job was a very wealthy man whom God smiled on. He was very blessed with loads of cattle, livestock, children, and land. Upon Satan questioning Job's obedience and loyalty to God, God granted Satan permission to take everything away from Job. However, God did not permit Satan to kill Job. Job lost everything; his livestock, his money, his kids, and his sense of self. Friends would ask him, "Job, why don't you give up, man?" His own wife told him to just "curse God and die". Job remains persistent in his pursuit toward God. He told his friends and wife that he did not need any of the things he had. "Naked (without possessions) came I [into this world] from my mother's womb, and naked (without possessions) shall I depart (Job 1:21). In the end, because of Job's will to bless God in the midst of his situation, God blessed him with twice as much as he had before. Job had way more money, livestock, land, children and the rest of his days were lived in peace and wellbeing. He stood on the promises of God and because of his faith God rewarded him.

Sometimes bad things happen to good people but it's up to us to hold on to the unchanging hand of God. Oftentimes God allows things to happen. God desires for our faith to be tested, our strength to be increased, and our wisdom to flourish. Like Job, remain prayerful, humble, and thankful when experiencing tough times. Please do not give up! Instead, pray and ask God for the strength to pull through. Hold on to that little voice in your head that gives you hope. For if you abide in Christ and stick close to God victory shall be yours.

Additional readings: (Psalms 31:24; Isaiah 41:10; Psalms 71:14)

1.   Complete this thought:

"When I feel weak I —————————————————"

"When I feel strong I ————————————————"

Reflect on how you feel when you release your problems to God verses holding onto things them.   What is the difference between both emotions?

Day 16

Starting Over

Philippians 3:13 "Brethren, I count not myself to have apprehended; but this one thing I do, forgetting those things which are behind and reaching forth unto those things which are ahead."

Starting over is one of the hardest things to do. The hurt you may have been enduring for a month or even longer could still feel like it only happened yesterday. It can seem demanding as it forces its way into your mind. I remember the dread in my stomach that I felt and the cringe look that I made every time I fathomed starting over.

Thankfully, with the help of God, I was able to make the decision to pick up the pieces of my life. I decided to use my past as a building block for my future. People say, "every setback is a set up for a comeback." This means that every time life seems to knock you down, it is really God's way of setting you up for His will to be done in your life. God comes to restore, support, and strengthen you. He then places you on a firm foundation so do not let your trials strangle you.

Instead, let it strengthen you. Let it be a chance for you to rediscover yourself and your purpose in God. Who knows? This could be the start of your women's ministry, nonprofit organization, or whatever plan God provides for you.

Go to God in prayer and fasting. Place Him at the center of your life and allow Him to shine a light into your future.

Additional reading (Isaiah 43:18; 2 Corinthians 5:17; Philippians 4:11)

1. What scares you the most about starting over? Analyze your fears and create an action plan for overcoming that feeling.

2. What do you know about your purpose? Do you know what it is? Figure out ways to work toward building your destiny.

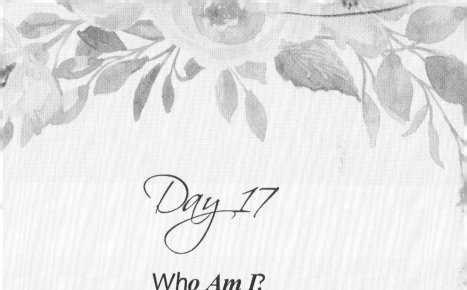

Day 17

Who Am I?

Psalms 10:1 "Why, O Lord, do you stand far away? Why do you hide yourself in times of trouble?"

"Why is this happening to me?" "Where was God when my marriage was falling apart?" These are some of the questions we ask ourselves. As the growing pains of life continues the nagging thoughts come rolling in. At some point, we may feel as though we have made progress and then out of nowhere we feel as though we're right back where it all began.

While separated, I discovered my identity was lost and could only define myself as a wife and a mother. I began searching for my identity in Jesus Christ and I encourage you to do the same. You are an individual who is fearfully and wonderfully made. Focus on finding who God created before placing you inside your mother's wound. You are more than just a "mother" and a "wife", you are a special individual capable of achieving great things. Depend solely on God and emancipate yourself from the pain and heartache that you have endured.

Guilt is an illusion designed to make you feel guilty of things that Jesus has freed you from.

When Job found himself in his darkest hours, he began to question God. He asked God some of the same questions we ask today. Deep down, you may wonder if God hears you or if you did something wrong to deserve all that you are going through. Just like Job, your faith will be tested. This is a chance for you to try God for yourself. Go to God and say, "Lord, I need you to give me the strength to get through this".

Additional reading: (Habakkuk 1:2; James 1:5; Corinthians 2:12)

1. What makes you think that you are not strong enough to make it through the toughest of times?

2. Make it a goal to trust God today, and every other day for the rest of your life.

Day 18

Conquering The Fear

2 Timothy 1:7 "For God hath not given us the spirit of fear, but of power and love and of a sound mind."

Fear is bred in environments of uncertainty. During this transition, you may experience different types of fear arising from different sources. You may fear having to start over and redefine yourself without your spouse. If you have children, you may fear how the separation will affect them in the long-run and let's not forget the unwanted opinions of friends and family.

Fear is of the enemy and not of God. It is a tool Satan uses to hinder you from the promises God has already made to you. Allowing fear to linger leads to having a lack of faith. It will cause you to doubt His sovereignty and lead to living outside of God's will. Today, decide to evict fear from your heart and mind. 1 John 4:18 reminds us that perfect love casts out all fear. Make a habit of focusing on God's truth and his unchanging hand. Walking by faith bounds up the spirit of fear and allows you to operate in obedience. When operating in obedience you'll be able to see the power of God working inside of your life. Instead of living in fear, choose to live in power under the guidance of the Holy Spirit. We learn to conquer fear by knowing and standing on the word of God. Choose to live in power and allow God to lead you.

Additional readings (Isaiah 35:4; Psalms 23:4; Psalms 34:4)

1. What scares you the most about change?

2. Think of a few practices that you can implement when you begin feeling fearful.

3. What scriptures help you overcome your fear?

Day 19

Finding Peace

John 14:27 *"Peace I leave with you, my peace I give to you; not as the world giveth, give I unto you. Let not your heart be troubled, neither let it be afraid."*

There is a reason that peace is listed as a fruit of the spirit. Life is stressful and our flesh is contrary to the temperament of God. We are quick to anger, prideful, unforgiving, and give into wickedness. If we were forced to depend on our own strength we would all be lost. Finding peace in the midst of all our internal chaos is not something that we can do without God. In fact, we cannot do anything without God.

God's plan for your life is worth finding peace for. We have to make a decision to live righteous according to God's word. Peace flows in the presence of the the Holy Spirit and the Holy Spirit lives inside of you. Always remember that it takes much less of a strain to let go and gain peace than it does to hold on to anger and gain chaos. While it is tough at times, all things must be forgiven so that our Father is able to forgive us.

Upset the enemy today by choosing to be joyful in the midst of what you are going through. Stand tall and shout songs of praise when your world becomes dark. Focus on all that God is doing for you despite all that is falling apart around you. This will remind you that you are covered by the hand of God. That you are the apple of His eye and this will bring you peace and confidence. Meditate on His words for comfort in this hour.

Additional reading: (Philippians 4:7; Job 22:21-22; Luke 2:13-14)

1. List a few scriptures that reassure you of God's perfect peace.

2. What are a few things that threaten your peace? Begin removing those things (or people) out of your life today.

Day 20

The Power Of Prayer

Jeremiah 29:12 "Then you will call on me and pray to me, and I will listen to you."

While prayer is essential to our lives, it can sometimes become a weapon that we try to use against each other. Instead of praying for forgiveness, protection, and redemption we go to God in anger and pray for vengeance we think that we deserve.

When my spouse and I separated, I began praying specifically for him. Lord, how did you create such a stupid man? Lord, fix him! Please fix him, Lord! It's not until I began praying for my heart to align with God's heart that transformation began to set in. God gave me a heart of flesh, renewed my mind, and gave me a peace I'd never experienced. I was able to walk through my separation with authority and power from God. The more you pray the more the enemy will use your spouse as a weapon. Whether it be money, kids, or things of the past but don't take your eyes off God. Ephesians 6:12 reminds us that we don't fight against flesh and blood but against the spirits of this world. The enemy works overtime to rip our families apart with the notion to kill, steal, and destroy. When we pray our prayers should be for continued strength, discernment, and forgiving hearts. We should ask the Lord to break every stronghold and up-root any tree of evil that has been planted in our lives. The enemy is against successful families because they bear witness to the love of God. It is important that we remember who our enemy truly is and go to war in prayer.

Additional readings: (James 5:13; Mark 11:24; Matthew 5:44)

1. What are some things that you are praying for or against right now?

2. Write down a prayer to recite every day in the morning as your personal declaration against the enemy.

Day 21

Your Children

Proverbs 22:6 "Train up a child in the way he should go; even when he is old, he will not depart from it."

Children are rarely the reason for a divorce to take place. During this time your main focus may be the emotional toll of your children. Divorce has no boundaries or limits to who it will and will not affect. Oftentimes, it may feel like they are only innocent characters in a film that are being inevitably played out before them.

Children sometimes blame themselves for the failed relationship or act out unnaturally because they don't know how to express their true feelings. During this time, it's very important to have consistent conversations with your children and allow them to express their emotions. You should help them, with guidance from the Holy Spirit, to sort through how they feel while encouraging love and forgiveness. When the enemy plants rejection or anger in the midst, teach them the significance of giving grace. It's important that you don't pin the children against the other parent and cause confusion. Confusion affects the children and places them in an awkward position of having to choose between the two parents. Do not panic when attempting to weigh these matters. If you have shared custody with your husband try to make it work and be there for your children.

Now, more than ever, your children need to feel your love. They have a way of sensing and internalizing the things that take place in their emotional environments. It is your responsibility to cleanse the air, pour into them daily, and feed them spiritually. Remind them of their value and reassure them that they are loved. Help them with school, social, and extracurricular activities. Remember that you are not the only one trying to heal. Divorce is a very traumatic experience for all parties involved.

Allow God to work through you to help them. He will provide you with a sense of balance and help you to move forward one step at a time. Trust God and ask Him to cover you and your children under His blood. I pray God provides healing and His hand of protection around you and your children. Amen.

Additional reading: (Psalms 127:3; Deuteronomy 6:7; Proverbs 29:17)

1. What are some ways that you can reassure your children that they are loved, seen, heard, and cared for even in the midst of your divorce?

2. How can you assure your child that you are paying attention to their needs during this time?

3. *Name some activities that you can do with your child or children.*

Day 22

Real Friends

Proverbs 17:17 "A friend loveth at all times, and a brother is born for adversity ."

When God completed His act of creation He reviewed His work and decided that it was not good for us to be alone. When Jesus later walked the earth, He demonstrated this yet again by choosing a group of over seventy men to go on a mission. Then, later distilling this list down to His twelve trusted friends; his disciples. None of these men were perfect yet they walked with Jesus and assisted Him when He performed miracles, signs, and wonders. One was so flawed that he betrayed Jesus and led Him to His death. Another disciple denied his relationship to Him and another doubted whether or not His resurrection was real.

Neither of these things caused Jesus to love them any less. He treated each man with respect and showed love equally among them. It is God's desire for us to have genuine friends in our lives. A good friend prays for you, builds you up in the word of God, and speaks life over your dead situations. God doesn't desire for us to just have anyone as a friend but he desires us to have a Godly friend. Job had friends who did not know how to give pep talks to him during his depressed time and Samson's girlfriend got him killed. Neither of these friendships are the kind that God wants us to have. He wants us to have fruitful relationships and abundant partnerships. We are encouraged not to neglect the fellowship of believers because iron sharpens iron. Real friends are essential in this rough time. David had Johnathan and Naomi had Ruth. These friendships changed bloodlines, made history, and saved lives because they were rooted in love, support, encouragement, and a reverence for God. May we all be blessed with a Godly community as we try to navigate this juncture of our lives.

Additional readings: (Proverbs 18:24; Proverbs 17:17; John 15:12-13)

1. List at least one good friend that you have. Write them a short note of appreciation.

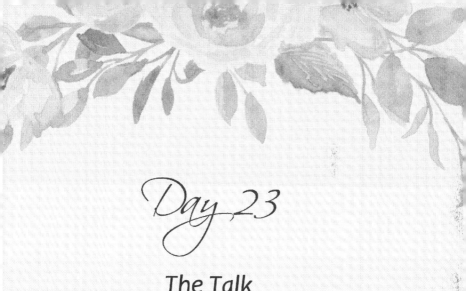

Day 23

The Talk

Proverbs 16:7 *"When a man's ways please the Lord, he maketh even his enemies to be at peace with him."*

This part is where it gets tricky. Talking to the one who broke your heart. It can be really stressful and difficult to do. Sometimes, for the sake of the kids and your own sanity, you have to break the silence. Making the first move does not mean you are weak. It means that you are prepared and strong enough to have a conversation concerning the most vulnerable parts of you. If you are able to look at your husband and genuinely wish them well, then you can be certain that God is moving you through the advanced stages of your healing and forgiveness. If you still find it hard, however, be patient with yourself. Forgiveness is not a one time thing. Actively work toward genuinely forgiving by releasing any ego or pride that you have within the situation and purposely release every weight that you feel to your Father God.

Human beings are obsessed with rushing things. Did you ever wonder how God remains so patient with us? Well, God transcends time and is not limited by it, so His patience supersedes ours. When you allow Him, God will patiently carve away the calluses formed around your heart. He then softens you to the point where you are strong in your vulnerability and confident in His grace. Celebrate your milestones when you are able to monitor the growth in your life and prayerfully increase your faith in God's favor. When you get to the point of having a conversation with your spouse and/or ex-spouse be sure to keep the past in the past. Allow conversations to remain level-headed and think before you speak. Resist the urge to be bitter, resentful, angry, or cold towards them and extend the love of Christ to them. Truly allow the peace of God to govern your heart before you have conversations and watch how God keeps you.

The standard that God holds His people to is that of royalty. We are a chosen generation and a holy people. We must forgive in paramount ways and carry ourselves as if we know that we ourselves have been forgiven by our Father God. While we suffer the same heartache as the world, we have a mighty God on our side. Let Him order your steps and show you His will for your life.

Additional readings: (Matthew 5:23-24; Ephesians 4:32; Romans 12:19)

1. What are some negative emotions that you can choose to release right now? What type of emotions will you place into your life to replace the negative ones?

2. List words and phrases that could trigger you and cause you anger during tough conversations. Be sure to remain aware of your triggers so that you can avoid acting out in ways that are unnatural and the opposite of peaceful.

Day 24

Believing In Yourself Again

Psalms 139:14 "I will praise thee, for I am fearfully and wonderfully made; marvelous are thy works and that my soul knoweth right well.

Going through a divorce or separation can definitely lower someone's self-esteem and often cause a person to second-guess themselves. As a Christian, you may feel like you have failed God somehow. You consider that maybe you should have prayed harder for your marriage to work or tried harder. Somewhere along the line, you start to believe all the negative things that have ever been said about you. God reminds us in His word that you are fearfully and wonderfully made. No mistake could ever make us less beautiful or less worthy in His sight. He knew us even before we were conceived and we are made perfectly in God's image. No one can define you, neither can your situation. Our definition comes solely from the one who created us, God. Only He has the authority to speak into our lives and tell us who we are and who we have been called to be.

When the devil whispers in your ear and tells you that you are unworthy, worthless, and unloved, shout back I'm worthy, important, and loved. Declare all that God says you are. Reflect on the scriptures for today and be encouraged. Be intentional about finding biblical affirmations for your life. Write out passages and leave them in visible places around your home. Believe in God as He helps you to believe in yourself again.

Additional readings: (Psalm 139:1; Rom. 5:5; Phil 4:13)

1. Write out a few biblical affirmations to guide you through your days and recite them frequently.

2. Name a few words that are the opposite of the negative feelings that you have. For example, if you feel like you are unworthy tell yourself "I am worthy".

Day 25

Loving Again

1 Corinthians 16:14 "Let everything that you do, be done in love."

When we get married, we never think that we will visit divorce. We never imagine ourselves readjusting our lives once we encounter the absence of our former spouse. It is one thing to drift away from your partner and then come back together but it is another thing to make your vows sound like a song filled with broken promises.

It is challenging to move on when you gave your everything to your marriage for it to end in divorce. However, when you decide to love yourself it makes all of the difference in the way that you become able to love others.

It is important to understand that God is love. Love is a feeling that cannot be explained, only experienced. Imagine what it would feel like to love yourself so unconditionally that freedom and forgiveness come easy to you. When you close your heart off you block the pathway to receiving the fullness of God.

Look around and you will discover that you are surrounded by love. If you allow yourself to experience it it can help restore your faith in God. You do not have to go seeking out another relationship immediately but you should not allow your divorce to rob you of God's gift of relationship to you.

You can love again and rebuild your idea of marriage by seeking wisdom and guidance from our Father God. Continue to pray for an overflow of God's love so love overflows from your heart into others. Love is patient, kind, humble, caring, and long suffering.

Additional reading (John 3:16; 1 John 4:16; Psalms 36:7)

1. What are a few ways that you can show love and acts of appreciation toward yourself this week?

2. How do you move on into the future if you do not have a plan for moving on from the past?

Day 26

Self-development

Philippians 4:13 "I can do all things through him who strengthens me."

When something so devastating as divorce happens we begin to criticize ourselves by failed works. In order for you to develop into who God called you to be you have to walk in righteousness. You may have not been the best person inside of your marriage but you're striving to be a better person moving forward. Regardless of what your spouse did we have to identify our wrong doings. It could be poor communication, bad attitude, showing anger instead of love, sarcasm and so forth but even if it was a response it's still considered wrong.

To grow internally, we have to take our struggles to God and allow Him to provide the strength that flows outwardly. Stop letting the pain of divorce cause you to stop taking care of yourself. Never let anything cause you to lose the essence of who God created you to be. Divorce should never be the reason that you stop growing. Things do not happen to us, they happen for us. In this new season of singleness, reconnect with God and strengthen the bond that exists between the two of you. God will help you to develop your consistency in areas that matter and you will have visible results. Overtime, God's hand on your life will become so obvious that you will be able to use your experience as a testimony for God.

Additional readings: (Philippians 4:13; 2Corinthians 5:17; Ephesians 4:22-24)

1. What do you feel is missing in your life? How will you work toward fixing this?

2. When was the last time you had a good laugh?

3. Describe your perfect day. Make a plan to bring that day to life.

Day 27

Find Your Purpose

Job 42:2 "I know that you can do all things, no purpose of yours can be thwarted."

The body of Christ is made up of individuals with multiple talents and gifts. The aim of the enemy is to distract us from using our gifts and talents to further the plan of God. The enemy is crafty in his distractions. His duty is to get you caught up in your plight and distracted by your pain. Then, he'll be able to rob the body of Christ of the gifts that are meant to be contributed towards God's plan. Instead of allowing this to happen team up with the Lord to fight the good fight. When we use this time to discover our gifts we will find ourselves refreshed and renewed as instruments of God.

Pray and ask God to help you discover His purpose for your life. Then, allow Him to mold you so that you can be a blessing to others. If your purpose does not align with the goals that you have created for yourself, scrape your plans and trust in God. His plan is greater than ours and He knows what is best for us. Allow God to work fully in your life so that you can have the greatest possible chance at the brightest future that is possible for you.

The Bible says, "For I know the plans I have for you, plans to prosper you and not harm you.

Plans to give you hope and a future". Let God show you what His hope is for your future.

Additional reading: (Jeremiah 29:11; Jeremiah 32:19; James 1:5)

1. Does your plan for your life align with the purpose that God has placed on the inside of you?

2. When you think of the feeling of love, what comes to mind? What do you visualize?

3. What obstacles to do often face the most? How can you overcome them?

Day 28

Watch God Work

Romans 15:13 "May the God of hope fill you with all joy and peace in believing, so that by the power of the Holy Spirit, you may abound in hope."

Having fun and enjoying life is possible after divorce. If "the joy of the Lord is your strength" as Nehemiah 8:10 states, life is fully capable of meaning more meaningful than it felt before. The love and peace of God equips us to do things that we could have never accomplished on our own. Like moving forward after divorce and living an enjoyable, fun life.

God does not want His people to be bogged down, depressed, and discouraged. His hope extends to all of us and He pulls us out from the depths of despair. When we become intentional in our outreach efforts whether to a neighbor, friend, or a stranger we are able to get more out of life. Once we selflessly learn to show love and grace, even when we feel that we ourselves have not received such treatment, we become exceedingly blessed by God. We are gifted with the ability to see life through multiple lenses making God's word appear more real to us through our daily experiences.

Try it today.

Make someone else your primary focus for this week and watch as God begins to move in your life. Be authentic in your efforts, be intentional in the ways that you show love, and watch God work in your life.

Additional reading (John 15:10-12; Psalms 16:11; Psalms 20:4-5)

1. Name 3 people that you can show love and appreciation for right now. Tell them you love them!

2. Think of a few random acts of kindness that you can show toward random strangers.

3. Release someone of a loan that they owe you. Trust that God will recompense you for what you have lost.

Day 29

The Restoration

Psalms 51:12 "Restore unto me the joy of thy salvation, and uphold me with thy free spirit."

Restoration can be defined as the act of returning something to its former state. Restoration can only begin with you. Once you make the decision to allow healing to fully take place within you, God begins working through you. It starts with you deciding that it is time for a change in your life. Through His grace and mercy you will be made new. It does not matter how long your marriage lasted or if your divorce happened years ago. God is the same today as He always has been. He remains the source of your strength and the only one who can save you. Thank God that restoration has no expiration date. God patiently awaits for you to return to Him with tender loving and kindness. Rest in knowing that God's plans for you are eternal. His love and His plan to save you is a promise that He has kept for all generations.

You are not too broken for God to fix and you are not too messed up for a spiritual restoration. God wants to perform miracles in your life.

While your intended blessings may not come when you want them to come but you will find that they arrive just in time. God will never go back on His word and He promises to never leave or forsake you. If you trust Him, He'll supernaturally restore you to where He needs you to be. He will begin to expose and remove toxic relationships while replacing them with relationships that will uplift you in His name.

Additional reading: (Jer. 30:17; Psalms 51:12; Isaiah 61:7)

1.   Name a few things that you are looking for God to do in your life this month. Write them down and pray over them. Have faith that God will accomplish the things that aligns with His plan for Your life. God can do great things in your life if you allow Him too.

Day 30

Breakthrough

Isaiah 60:1 "Arise shine for your light has come, and the glory of the Lord rises upon you."

The moment of breakthrough is a feeling that cannot be described in words. It feels like you have finally made it out of the fire and into your best days to come. At the point of breakthrough, believing in yourself seems possible again. It is at the point that you and God are able to finally move forward. When you encounter a breakthrough, it is only because you have decided to release the past, let go of bitterness, and completely show forgiveness in the situations that you have encountered. You have finally decided to love yourself and focus on rebuilding your life with God. A breakthrough lies on the other end of your obedience, and your obedience is crucial to the work that God wants to do in your life.

God is all powerful however He will never force Himself pass your own desires of freewill. We have a significant role to play in our breakthrough process. While we

73

cannot heal ourselves we must participate in the healing process. Even if that means having uncontrollable spells of tears at the most inconvenient times. We cannot reach inside of ourselves and pull out the already healed versions of ourselves. We must work towards it every single day. God stands by our side and helps us through our trials. He heals, delivers, and set free.

If you decide today that you want to experience a breakthrough you can call upon the divine formula. It involves earnest prayer, fervent faith, vulnerability, quiet moments with God, and obedience to His will. After seemingly carrying the weight of the world on your shoulders you deserve the rest that comes from being obedient to God's word.

My prayer is that as we all go through our journeys we will find God to be the rock that He says He is. We will come out of our breakthroughs believing that God is eternally unfailing and always there for us during our good times and our times of need. In Jesus Holy Name Amen.

Additional reading (Isaiah 60 1-22; John 8:32)

1. Who was I when I first began this journal? How have I changed?

2. What are my goals for moving forward for the rest of the year?

AFTERTHOUGHT

Words of Encouragement

Now that we've come to an end of this journey together but into a new beginning I pray that you are encouraged knowing that you are not alone. You are not the first person to experience separation and/or divorce and you will not be the last. As long as you are still breathing, know that this life is filled with unexpected curveballs, twists, and turns. All things are working together to create the grand plan that God has for each of us in the long run. If you allow yourself to let go, forgive, and heal you'll eventually look back on these days and show appreciation to yourself for never giving up. Learn how to show gratitude every single day even when days seem hard. Watch how your mind is transformed from seeing the worse to only perceiving the best in every situation.

Allow God to be the center of your joy and watch how His strength is made perfect in your weakness. Learn how to be alone and comfortable in your own skin without feeling lonely. Read your Bible and learn how different individuals made it through their most depressed times. While it may seem like people in the Bible were more heroic or had more faith than you do, understand that you, too, will make it through your toughest moments if you only believe in God.

God created you to be strong and durable; you are built to last. Stand up in your freedom to be who God called you to be and walk boldly into your future. Do not be afraid. Fear is of the enemy. Break past feelings of fear and doubt and seek God's face for help. Be confident in who God says you are and find courage from knowing that God promised He will never leave nor forsake you.

Your life is not over just because you have experienced a divorce. Your new life is just beginning and you will embark on the exploration of a lifetime as God leads and guides you into who you were created to be. I Pray God overflows your heart with His love and overwhelms you with His presence. I am happy for you, I believe in you, and I am excited for you!!! IN JESUS NAME, AMEN!!!

Made in the USA
Middletown, DE
28 July 2021